Cra

Louise

Some other books of fun published in Armada

2nd Armada book of Jokes and Riddles
compiled by Jonathan Clements

The Awful Joke Book
The Even More Awful Joke Book
The Most Awful Joke Book Ever
The Funniest Funbook
The Batty Book Book
compiled by Mary Danby

The Whizzkid's Handbook
The Whizzkid's Handbook 2
The Whizzkid's Handbook 3
The Secret Agent's Handbook
The Spookster's Handbook
by Peter Eldin

Crazy – But True!

by Jonathan Clements

Illustrated by Roger Smith

This edition of *Crazy – But True!*,
first published in 1986 in Armada by Fontana Paperbacks,
8 Grafton Street, London W1X 3LA,
contains material from *Crazy – But True!* (1974),
More Crazy – But True! (1976) and
The Day It Rained Mashed Potato (1978).

Armada is an imprint of Fontana Paperbacks,
a division of the Collins Publishing Group.

Printed in Great Britain by
William Collins Sons & Co Ltd, Glasgow

Ham and Eggs

In 1974, a thousand pigs went berserk near Devizes, in Wiltshire. They ate the fabric of a light aeroplane, seven wooden gates, 2½ tons of hay, a straw rick, 10 cwt of cattle cake, 500 yards of electric wire, and 17 acres of cabbages.

A Victorian poetess named Nancy Luce loved her chickens so much that they were the only things she ever wrote about. What's more, she inscribed her poems on the chickens' eggs, and it's thought that she wrote at least 100,000 chicken poems. Not suprisingly, none of the poems survived.

An ostrich egg takes approximately forty minutes to softboil. And an hour and a half to hard-boil.

Creepy Crawlies

Garden midges beat their wings approximately one thousand times a second.

Only the female mosquito bites: the male of the species is not equipped for biting.

The common silkworm has eleven brains. But it only uses five of them.

The common garden wood-louse (which can roll itself into a tight ball) used to be given by medieval doctors to patients suffering from gout or palsy.

There are approximately five hundred million spiders in Great Britain.

Earthworms more than 2 metres long are to be found in some parts of Western Australia.

The three body segments of an insect do not depend on one another for survival. Thus an insect whose head has been cut off may live as long as a year in this condition.

Long and Short

The smallest and the tallest people in the world live in Africa. The men of the Batutsi tribe average 7 feet 4 inches (2.24m.) in height—and the men of the Pygmy tribe grow to an average of 4 feet 1 inch (1.25m.).

An 8-foot (2.45m.) tall giant, Thomas Jenkins, a clerk at the Bank of England, who died in 1798, requested that to foil body-snatchers he be buried in the safest place he knew—on the Bank's premises. His wish was carried out, and Jenkins's corpse is still there today.

Attila the Hun, leader of the hordes of Barbarians who overran much of Europe, was a dwarf, just 3 feet 4 inches (1.02m.) tall.

What a sweet little Hun

Actually I'm a little Horror!

ATTILA'S A KILLER

Mad Motorists

In April, 1906, a head-on collision occured in Redruth, Cornwall. So what? The accident was between the only two cars existing in the town at the time.

The first person caught in Oslo's computer-radar-speed-assessor-trap, in 1982, was Police Chief Johan Gerde.

A salesman who admitted a speeding offence wrote to Wigan magistrates, explaining that his speedometer had been steamed up by the hot black puddings he was carrying at the time. He was fined £10.

Motorist Phillip Cathie of Hove, Sussex, was caught reversing his car up a one-way street. A somewhat lenient magistrate fined him the sum of one penny for his crime.

Right and Wrong

In one of Elvis Presley's school reports, a teacher wrote: "This boy is terrible: he can't sing a note, is tone-deaf, and couldn't carry a tune to save his life. It would be a merciful thing for everybody if Elvis Presley stopped having music lessons."

The scientist Hegel published his proof that there could be no more than seven planets just a week before the discovery of the eighth.

The American writer Mark Twain (real name Samuel Leghorn Clemens) was born in 1834, the time when Halley's Comet had just been sighted and was front-page news all over the world. Later, Twain commented in an article: "I came in with the Comet, and I expect to go out with it." Mark Twain died in 1910, just a few days before the reappearance of the Comet.

Jehovah's Witnesses predicted that the world would end during the summer of 1984. They were wrong; it didn't.

When a submarine was invented by Dutchman Cornelius van Drebel, in 1624, the British Admiralty scoffed at the invention, and are on record as saying that it was "a damn silly, trifling novelty that will never catch on".

Tall Story

When the American Army Corps of Engineers took over construction of the Washington Monument in 1880, they were faced with a seemingly insoluble problem: since there had been no work done on the project in twenty-five years, the ropes and scaffolding leading to the top of the monument had rotted with age. If additional bricks and mortar were to be hauled to the top, the ropes would have to be replaced, but nobody had any idea how to get the ropes to the top. The whole project seemed stymied before it had begun.

Then some bright spark had a brainstorm. Inside the 48-metre-high hollow shaft, a wire was tied to the leg of a pigeon. A gun was fired, and the frightened bird flew skyward, where it was killed with a blast from a second gun. The poor pigeon fell to the ground, still tied to the wire, which the engineers then used to haul up heavier cables and, ultimately, the scaffolding needed to complete the job.

Quirky Queens

Queen Elizabeth I created an office called "The Official Uncorker Of Sea-Bottles", after a fisherman in Cornwall found an important official secret in a bottle washed up on the beach. Any person not handing over such bottles to the Officer was liable to be hanged.

The most costly dress ever made was worn by Marie de Medici, Queen of France, in 1622. The dress was embroidered with 3,000 diamonds and 39,000 pearls—at today's values it would be worth £6,000,000. The Queen only wore the dress once, then discarded it.

During her life, Queen Victoria would never allow the royal train to exceed 30 mph. (Once, when travelling from London to Brighton, the train reached the speed of 40 mph. When she found out, the Queen had the driver whipped and sacked from his job.) However, when, in 1901, Queen Victoria's body was brought from the Isle of Wight to Windsor, the train from Southampton touched 95 mph, and rocked violently on some of the curves.

Rum Reds

One morning in 1798, as Czar Paul I of Russia was inspecting his guards, he was infuriated by a soldier's cloak button, which hadn't been polished. In a rage the Czar ordered: "About turn—march!" When asked where to, he shouted: "To Siberia!"

The 400 men dutifully set off on the 2,000 mile march—and were never heard of again.

When the Russian writer Tolstoy (author of *War and Peace*) was a boy, he formed an exclusive club with his brother. To be initiated, a member had to stand in a corner of the room for an hour and not think of a white bear.

In 1821, Maria Feodorewna, wife of Alexander I of Russia, accidentally caught sight of a note pinned to the bottom of a death-warrant. It was in the handwriting of her husband, and read: "Pardon impossible, to be sent to Siberia." Maria kindly transposed the comma so that it read: "Pardon, impossible to be sent to Siberia." Whereupon the lucky convict was released, a free man.

You Don't Say!

Alfred Nobel initiated and sponsored the famous Nobel Peace Prize. Before that, he was best known as the inventor of dynamite.

On board the Russian spaceship, Salyut 6, launched in 1980, was a black-and-white teddy bear named Mishka.

In 1770, a Bill was introduced in Parliament, "denouncing women who wrongly seduce men into marriage by the use of costly scents, paints, cosmetic washes, artificial limbs, false hair, false teeth, iron stays and corsets, hoops, high-heeled shoes, and bolstered bosoms and hips."

If a woman was convicted of capturing a husband by any of these means, the marriage would be declared null and void. The Bill never did become law—fortunately for the state of matrimony. For there cannot have been a single wife who did not resort to at least one of the crimes listed!

Birds of a Feather

At a 1984 Nottingham exhibition entitled "Vanishing Wildlife", somebody stole a stuffed owl.

Woodpecker scalps were highly prized by North American Indian tribes—one was enough to buy a wife with.

The Australian bush-turkey collects about five tons of leaves and twigs to build its huge nest.

The owl is the only creature able to turn its head in a complete circle.

In Hawkshead, Lancashire, there is a well-known pub called "The Drunken Duck". Its unusual name derives from an incident that occurred there in 1788. One summer's day, beer seeped from the pub's cellar into the ducks' feed trough. The landlady found the ducks apparently dead, and she started plucking them and preparing them for the oven. Suddenly, the ducks started sobering up. The somewhat eccentric landlady made amends by knitting small graments for the naked ducks to wear.

Fancy That!

In 1983, art lovers at the Serpentine Gallery in Kensington Gardens, London, were amazed to discover the Arts Council had paid £7,000 for an exhibit which featured a tray of animal droppings.

A complete copy of "The Rubaiyat of Omar Khayyam", measuring just ⁵⁄₁₆ of an inch square, was made by James Featherstone of Yorkshire.

The motto of the peace-loving Salvation Army is "Blood and Fire!"

Ju-jitsu, literally translated into English, means "The gentle art".

Yum-Yum!

One of the worst drinks in the world must be a wine called Moam, which is drunk in Indonesia. It is made from mashed-up snakes and sugar.

The Chinese emperor, Ch'eng Tung, ordered his chief minister, I Yin, to prepare an inventory of the most tasty foods available in all the world. I Yin's selections, compiled in the year 1500 BC, included the following:

The lips from the orang-outan ape.
The tails of young swallows.
The knees of the elephant.
The tail of the yak.
The blue mushrooms from the Yang-hua valley.
Sardines from the Eastern sea.
Duckweed from rivers sheltered by yew trees.
Sauce made from sturgeon, leeks, cinnamon and lichens.

Pachyderm Party

The elephant is the only animal that cannot jump.

An eleven year-old elephant named Batyr, living now in Karaganda Zoo, Russia, can put the end of his trunk in his mouth and talk. Since he started this trick in 1980, his vocabulary has grown to over 200 words.

An elephant's trunk can carry 2 gallons of water.

Drunken elephants are quite a big problem in South Africa's Kruger National Park. It seems that they are particularly fond of the sweet fruits of the marula tree, which thrives within the park's boundaries. After a feast of marula fruit an elephant becomes terrifically thirsty and wanders off to the nearest stream to fill up on gallons of water. Intestinal fermentation then converts the fruit sugars to alcohol and leaves the giant animal thoroughly drunk. You can hear a drunken elephant from miles away; it trumpets wildly like a highly-amplified pop-group. Furthermore, a tipsy elephant loses all its inhibitions; it stampedes, squashing other animals, staggers about, and finally collapses in a stupor.

Anyone for squash?

Well I Never!

Rabbits have been known to reach a speed of 47 m.p.h.

The engineers of the M5 Motorway to Exeter built the smallest underpass in the world—a tunnel one foot wide to allow badgers to get safely to the other side.

A special penknife made in 1822 by Joseph Rodgers & Sons Ltd of Sheffield, Yorkshire, had 1,822 blades. One blade was added every year up until 1973, when a total of 1,973 blades left no room for any more.

Fishing for Worms

A somewhat drastic cure for tapeworms was invented by Dr Alpheus Meyers, of Sheffield, Yorkshire, in 1877. His patent "Tapeworm Trap" was a small metal cylinder, tied to a string and baited with food, which the patient swallowed after fasting long enough to work up the worm's appetite. Naturally, the tapeworm would poke its head into one end of the cylinder, where it would be caught by a metal spring strong enough to hold it tight, but not so strong that it would decapitate it.

With the quarry thus trapped, the attending physicians would grasp the end of the string hanging from the patient's mouth and haul up the trap, parasite and all.

A good idea—but after several people had choked to death using the contraption, it was suggested to Dr Meyers that perhaps his true vocation really lay in the invention of angling equipment.

Stamp! Stamp! Stamp!

When Rowland Hill first had the idea of a "piece of paper just large enough to bear the Crown's stamp, and covered at the back with a kind of glue, with which the bringer might, by applying a little moisture, attach it to the front of a letter", he met with a great deal of opposition. The then Postmaster General, Lord Lichfield, publicly expressed his disapproval of the idea thus:

"Why, of all the wild, crackpot and idiotic schemes I have ever heard of, this is the most foolish and extravagant! The man Hill should be horse-whipped!"

A banana-shaped stamp was issued in Tonga in 1974.

The first pop star to appear on a postage stamp was Michael Jackson—on a British Virgin Islands set in 1985.

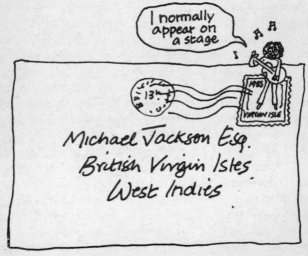

Who's Chicken?

Over the course of several weeks in 1971, about nine hundred people in the neighbouring villages of Mbale and Kigezi, Uganda, were seized by a mad compulsion to run wildly through the streets, clutching chickens and screaming until they collapsed from exhaustion. Local natives attributed the mania to the will of dead village chieftains. However, scientists and psychologists diagnosed it as a case of mass hysteria, comparable to a laughing epidemic which had overrun the town of Bukoba, Tanzania, the previous year.

One of the earliest recorded cases of mass hysteria was that of the "biting nuns". At a convent in Germany in the fifteenth century, several nuns mysteriously began nipping at each other. Soon this "nun-biting" spread to other convents in Germany, and ultimately to convents in Holland and Italy.

Barmy Behaviour

The eighteenth century Gloucester eccentric, Charles Hamilton, apparently considered it a mark of esteem to have a real live hermit living in his garden. He offered handsome wages for the service, including a salary of £700 a year (equivalent to £7,000 today), and such valuable perks as a hair-shirt, an hour-glass, a rough sacking bed, and a Bible. In return, the hired hermit was expected to live in an artificial cave, not speak, and leave hair, nails and beard untrimmed. The one hermit Hamilton was able to lure into the position nearly went mad with boredom after six weeks, however, and ran away. A fellow-countryman of Hamilton's in Gloucester, though, had better luck, maintaining a hermit in a cave for nearly four years, but only on condition that the hermit be supplied with books, a bath-tub and a steam organ.

YOU ARE FORBIDDEN TO SPEAK TO THE HERMIT

Feeling a temptation to neglect his scholarly duties, the Greek philosopher Demosthenes shaved one side of his head, so he'd feel too humiliated to be seen in public.

In a crying contest in New York, Verne Sandusky cried for 3½ hours, producing nearly half a pint of tears.

Edward VII used to weigh his guests after weekends at Sandringham, to make sure they had eaten well and gained weight.

Major George Hanger, friend of the Prince Regent, once rode his horse up the stairs and into the attic of the house belonging to the fastidious Mrs Fitzherbert in Brighton. It needed eleven men, a crane and pulley and a blacksmith to get it down again. On another occasion, the madcap major harnessed a bull weighing four and a half tons and rode it up and down the Promenade at Brighton, much to the consternation of passers-by, many of whom fled into the sea.

Loose Limbs

Scottish surgeon Robert Liston was known for his speed and recklessness. Once, in 1841, he amputated a patient's leg in just forty-two seconds—unfortunately he did it so quickly that he also sawed off three of his assistant's fingers.

The Marquis of Anglesey had his leg amputated after an injury in the Battle of Waterloo. The leg was buried with full military honours in a nearby garden, with the Marquis proudly looking on. A hundred years later, the occupant of the cottage was still showing the grave as a tourist attraction, charging a halfpenny a look.

There is no cork in the artificial leg known as a cork leg. The name comes from Dr Cork, who invented them.

Fleas and Flies

Jumping beans have real live fleas inside them.

Egyptian slaves were ordered by their masters to smear themselves with the cream of camels' milk and honey, and then sit close to their masters to draw the flies from them.

A flea can jump 200 times its own height.

A fly's wings vibrate 340 times a second.

Love and Marriage

Brigham. Young, American Mormon leader, once married four women in one day.

Sir Walter Raleigh's widow carried her husband's embalmed head wherever she travelled until she died, nearly 29 years after Sir Walter's execution.

In 1967, a Prague housewife, Vera Czemsk, jumped out of her sixth-storey bedroom window when she learned that her husband was planning to run away from her. She recovered in hospital after landing on top of her husband—who was killed outright.

Each of the six husbands of Fram Irmgard Bruns, who lived in Berlin in the 1800s, committed suicide.

In 1968, an Austrian anthropologist named Hans Weizl lived for some months among the natives of northern Siberia. Throughout his stay he was constantly pestered by giggling young teenage girls, who would appear at his door and pelt him with handfuls of lice and slugs, day and night. After a while, Weizl learned that among the northern Siberians lice and slug-throwing is the traditional manner for a woman to express her love for a man, and indicates that she is available for marriage. (It makes you wonder what on earth they throw if they don't like you.)

Loony Looting

In 1982, a man stole a woman's false leg and held it to ransom for £100. Police in Aberdeen, where the man lived, caught him.

A criminal was arrested and found guilty in Harlow, Essex, of stealing over 800 Bus-Stop signs.

In 1983, a Sydney police station in Australia had all the brass fixtures and fittings stolen from their lavatories.

Sickly Sovereigns

George IV of England's cause of death was officially recorded as: rupture of the stomach blood vessels; alcholic cirrhosis; gout; nephritis, and dropsy.

In February, 1685, King Charles II died of a stroke—or so say his official biographers. In truth, it was probably the treatment for the stroke that did him in. On the morning of the stroke, twelve physicians were summoned to the royal chambers, and they immediately started to purge all the poisons from the king's body. First they relieved him of a quart of blood, then shaved his scalp and singed it with redhot irons. Then they filled his nose with sneezing powder and blanketed him with hot plasters, which they then tore off. The treatment produced no results, and Charles sank quickly. Frantically, the doctors bombed the monarch with more bleedings, purgatives, and fed him with mysterious potions learnt from ancient books—powdered horse's skull, pearls dissolved in ammonia, the skin of frogs, rooks' feathers soaked in ass's milk . . . but nothing worked. On the fifth day, after quietly apologising for taking so long to die, Charles breathed his last—perhaps with some relief.

That was a stroke of bad luck for us

Weird Warblings

Every year the British Wildlife Recording Society holds a competition to select the finest natural soundtracks in a variety of categories. For example, in 1972, Ray Goodwin of Gloucestershire won the coveted award for "Most Unusual Entry" with his tape of "A Roman Snail Chewing a Lettuce Leaf". This was highly amplified, sounding, as one reporter put it, "like a series of booming, crunching, ear-shattering noises lasting about two minutes."

Among other Goodwin recordings that have won prizes are recordings of "A Dung Beetle at Play", and "A Pair of Butterflies Fighting".

The winner of the Mammal division in 1974 was Arthur Acland, a seventy-year-old retired underwear salesman from Kent, with his irresistible entry: "A Humorous Recording of a Hedgehog Barking to Warn Off Other Spiny Members of his Tribe as He Sips a Bowl of Milk".

Did You Know . . ?

The Daimler "Conquest" car owed its name to its original price, before purchase tax, of £1,066. (1066 was the date of the Norman Conquest.)

In Japan, only members of the Japanese Imperial Family are allowed to use a maroon-coloured car.

Alan Jay Lerner took two weeks to write the last line of the song "Wouldn't It Be Loverly?" for the show *My Fair Lady*. The words of the last line are: "Loverly, loverly, loverly, loverly."

In Hollywood, some sets used as backgrounds in Western films are made to three-quarters scale, so as to make the heroes seem larger than life.

Crime and Punishment

In 1897, while serving a sentence in the Ohio State Penitentiary, a prisoner named Charles Justice helped design, build and install its first electric chair. Years later, he returned to the prison after being convicted of murder, and in 1911 was executed in that same electric chair.

Three men were hanged, for the murder of a magistrate, on Greenberry Hill, London, in 1641. Their names were Green, Berry and Hill.

In New Delhi, India, it is illegal to ride a bicycle at more than 65m.p.h., or to walk backwards after sunset.

You can be jailed in Brussels for not killing furry caterpillars when you have the chance. (The sentence would be from one to seven days.)

In Kelsey Park, Beckenham, Kent, you may not, according to a sign displaying ancient bye-laws, do any of the following things: play a musical instrument, shake out your mats or carpets, practise gymnastics, drive a horse-drawn bus.

Nor, if you happen to be "infested with vermin", may you "lie about by day" in the park.

Sir Charles Mompesson, found guilty in 1632 of blackmail, arson, cruelty and threatening tradesmen, was sentenced to the following: to lose his knighthood, pay a £10,000 fine, suffer a hundred strokes of the whip, forfeit his property and valuables, walk down the Strand with his face to a horse's tail, held forever to be an infamous rogue—and then to be imprisoned for life. However, through an underground system of bribery and corruption, Sir Charles was pardoned.

Would You Believe It?

To illustrate a lecture on marine biology at St John's College, Minnesota, U.S.A., Professor Daniel Kaiser swallowed 257 live minnows.

The average man spends 3,500 hours of his life on shaving. In this time, he removes about 30 ft of whiskers off his face.

When James Heatherington invented and wore the very first top hat in London, on January 5th, 1797, women fainted and young children screamed with alarm. So great was the commotion brought about by Heatherington's revolutionary headgear that he found himself summoned to appear before the Lord Mayor. He was bound over to keep the peace for the sum of £50, having been adjudged guilty of "appearing on a public highway wearing upon his head a tall structure having a shiny lustre and calculated to terrify people, frighten horses and disturb the balance of society".

Saints Alive!

St Wilgefortis was one of nine sisters born to an infidel king of Portugal. At an early age, Wilgefortis was converted to Christianity and took a vow of chastity, in spite of which her father betrothed her to the King of Sicily. The young girl prayed fervently for deliverance from the clutches of the Sicilian, and miraculously, on the day of her wedding, she sprouted a full black beard and moustache. Her fiancé lost interest. Her father, in a mad rage, had her crucified.

St Wilgefortis is traditionally invoked in the prayers of maidens who wish to be rid of unwanted boyfriends. In Britain, she is known as "St Uncumber", prayed to by women who wish to unencumber themselves of husbands they do not love.

St Andrew, Scotland's patron saint, wasn't a Scot at all. He was a Pict, a race that was regarded as Scotland's greatest enemy.

Nasal News

Ruth Clarke, of Mansfield, kept a yellow tiddlywink up her nose for twenty years. Recently she had an operation for sinus trouble, and the surgeon was amazed to discover the reason for the discomfort was the tiddlywink. Miss Clarke, now 25 years old, is reported to have said: "I loved tiddlywinks when I was 5, but I don't remember losing a yellow one . . ."

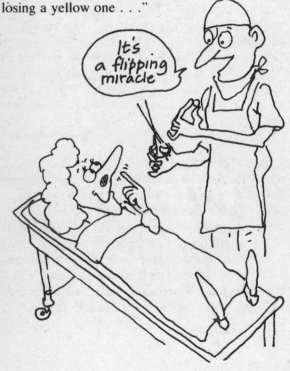

15-year-old Sayuri Tanaka of Japan was said in 1983 to have a third eye—apparently she can see with her *nose*. Even when blindfolded, she can still continue to read.

While studying at the University of Rostock, the Danish astronomer Tycho Brahe was insulted by a fellow student, and promptly challenged him to a duel. In the following contest, Brahe's nose was sliced off with a sword. Noseless, he commissioned a jeweller to make him a brilliant new nose out of gold and silver, which he wore for the rest of his life. The man with the golden nose is best remembered for his precise observations of the heavens, which paved the way for the discoveries of Kepler and Newton. The largest crater on the moon is named in Tycho's honour.

Henry Lewis, a Liverpool billard player, used to play with his nose instead of a cue. In 1928, he made a break of 46 points in this way.

Not What They Seem

Holidaymakers by the sea often praise the healthy ozone in the air. They're mistaken—what they can smell is just decaying seaweed. Ozone isn't present below an altitude of seven thousand feet.

Sealing wax contains no wax. It is made of shellac, turpentine, and cinnabar.

Snow isn't white—it's transparent. It is composed of tiny crystals, each with six sides. The rays of light, reflected by the various surfaces, give snow its impression of glistening whiteness.

There is no lead in a lead pencil. The material used is either plumbago or graphite, a form of carbon.

How Amazing!

The first recorded appearance of slot-machines was in the ancient temples of Alexandria. There were machines there from which a supply of Holy Water could be obtained when a coin was inserted in them—this was back in 641 BC.

The female starfish produces 2 million eggs a year. Ninety-nine per cent of them are eaten by other fish.

In Pas de Calais, France, there is a river named "Aa".

The first Duke of Marlborough was allergic to cabbage.

French Fancies

King Louis XIV of France originated and was the first to wear high-heeled shoes.

Actually he's just a big heel

The longest sentence ever published appears in Victor Hugo's *Les Misérables*. It is 823 words long and takes up over three pages.

Hugo, among others, also wrote the shortest letter on record. While on holiday, he was anxious to find out how *Les Misérables* was selling. To his Paris publishers he wrote: "?" The reply was "!".

In the eight years between 1601 and 1609, two thousand French noblemen died whilst fighting duels.

There is a small village in France named "Y".

Y

Why?

Goodness Gracious!

Circus tights were invented by an American bare-back rider, Nelson Hower, in 1828, when he appeared in his underwear after his costume failed to arrive. The fashion caught on.

When the first escalators at a tube station were installed at Earls Court in 1911, the general public were too scared to use them. So London Transport employed a man with a wooden leg to ride up and down on the escalator all day long, to prove that they were quite safe. His wages were 15p a day.

Mice can actually sing. Their songs, when magnified, resemble the twitterings of a canary, and are very musical.

On the Throne

King Charles II, who ruled from 1660 to 1685, was in the habit of gathering up dust and powder from the mummies of Egyptian kings and rubbing it all over himself. "I do this," he said, "to help me acquire ancient greatness."

Richard I (the Lionheart) spent only four months of his life in England.

George I, King of England from 1714 to 1727, was German and couldn't speak a word of English.

Queen Anne (1702-1774) bore a total of 17 children . . .

Queen Anne (The Great Bore of England)

Henry VIII's second wife, Anne Boleyn, always wore gloves to hide an odd physical deformity. She had six fingers on her left hand.

King Charles I was only 4 feet 7 inches (1.4m.) tall.

and outlived every one of them.

managed to bore her 17 children to death

A-tishoo!

If your doctor tells you you're suffering from acute nasopharyngitis, don't worry. That's the scientific name for the common cold.

In 1979, 12 year-old Patricia Raey of Liverpool caught a cold and continued sneezing for a further 194 days before she thankfully stopped.

The initial wind velocity of a human sneeze is more than Gale Force 10.

The common cold is estimated to cost the world's economy more than ten thousand million pounds a year in lost work time.

Peculiar Punishments

In 1973, a Manchester magistrate sentenced a pickpocket to three months in jail for stealing £5 from a woman's handbag. Noting the defendant's record of twenty-five previous convictions, the magistrate also ordered the man to wear enormous fur gloves whenever he appeared in public for the next two years. However, the pickpocket, after serving his three months, disappeared.

Across the ocean, Pierre Morganti, the mayor of Olistro on the island of Corsica, announced in the summer of 1976 that anybody caught sunbathing in the nude on the beach there would be painted blue. Seven people were punished thus.

In nearby Linguizetta, the town council, adopting the example of Lady Godiva, punishes minor offenders by making them ride naked through the streets on a donkey.

B. C. Bods

Julius Caesar wasn't a Roman Emperor—in fact there was no Roman Empire till a long time after his death. He was Consul five times, and became a Dictator.

"Aesop's Fables" weren't written by Aesop. Aesop was a deformed Phrygian slave of the 6th century B.C. Many of the fables attributed to him have been discovered on Egyptian papyre of 1,000 years earlier.

The word "Eureka" (which is Greek for "I've found it!") became famous when used by the mathematician Archimedes on discovering the principle that bodies can be weighed according to their displacement of water. The tradition is that Archimedes made his dramatic discovery when he stepped into his bath one day and observed the water overflowing. He immediately bolted out into the street, crying "Eureka! Eureka!" Thus Archimedes not only discovered that important principle—he also inadvertently invented streaking.

The first organised "strike" of workers dates back to 309 B.C. Then Aristos, a Greek musician, called out his orchestra because they weren't allowed to have their meals in the temple.

Cleopatra's Needle, on the Victoria Embankment in London, has nothing whatsoever to do with Cleopatra. Hieroglyphics, carved on the obelisk, tell that it was first erected in Egypt in 1475 B.C.—over 14 centuries before Cleopatra was born.

Heavenly Hot-Pot

The town of King's Lynn, in Norfolk, was hit by a freak snow-storm in August, 1973. But on closer inspection the white flakes bore a striking resemblance to mashed potato. It turned out that they actually *were* mashed potato, in instant form, and the white flakes covered cars and houses—and even turned black cats white.

The cause of the potato-flake storm was a malfunctioning machine in a local factory. Instead of pouring a mashed potato mixture into little bags, the machine was discharging the substance into the air in great quantities. The instant potato then soared up into the clouds, all fifty tons of it, and, when shortly afterwards it rained, the flakes were distributed over a wide area.

Odd Bodies

The human body contains enough phosphorous to make two thousand matchheads, sufficient iron to make a 15cm. nail, and enough fat to make eight bars of soap.

Most people think the heart is on the left side of the body. It isn't. Nine-tenths of it is on the right side.

There are twelve million cells in the human brain.

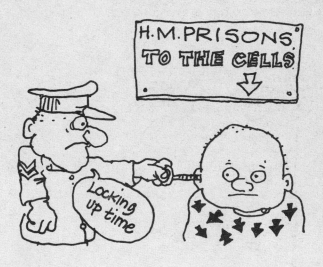

There are no such things as double-joints. Limbs that possess very flexible qualities are merely the result of stretched ligaments.

B-r-r-r!

Only one in fifty Eskimos has even seen an igloo, let alone lived in one.

Snowflakes measuring 17 inches across fell in Montana, U.S.A., in February 1887.

Most Eskimos use refrigerators—to keep their food from freezing.

The average iceberg weighs twenty million tons.

Toothy Tales

The very first set of false teeth was made of wood (elm) and was worn by George Washington.

Martin Van Butchell, "Tooth-Drawer and Corn-Curer", travelled around the streets of London in the middle of the eighteenth century. Somewhat eccentric by nature, Butchell rode on a small pony painted with bright red spots ("so people can see me coming"), with a small blind let down over its eyes ("to prevent the stupid animal from panicking"). His charges, though, were reasonable: twopence halfpenny for extracting a tooth, and one penny for curing a corn. He would also perform the service of plucking chickens, charging a penny halfpenny a dozen. Butchell always carried with him a large bone—said to be the thigh-bone of a horse—to protect himself against the thieves and rogues of London.

Animal Oddities

A chimpanzee living at Regent's Park Zoo, London, by the name of Congo, has painted over 250 pictures. Some of them have been sold to admiring tourists.

Lions used to be kept (like ferocious guard-dogs) in the Tower of London up till 1781.

The giraffe has the same number of bones in its neck as a human being.

The rhinoceros's horn isn't horn at all. It's made of hair so compact that it's as hard as bone.

A herd of springboks containing an estimated 100 million animals was seen in South Africa in 1896.

All golden hamsters are descendants of a single wild family found near Aleppo, in Syria, some forty years ago.

Gorillas can't swim.

Oil and Vinegar

One ounce of oil can cover an area of 8 acres with a fine film—that's over 32,000 square metres.

The Vinegar River (El Rio Vinagre) in Colombia contains eleven parts of sulphuric acid and nine parts of hydrochloric acid in every thousand, and is so bitter that no fish can live in it.

The reason sardines are crammed so tightly into their tins is that the oil used to pack them is more expensive by volume than the fish themselves. Thus, the more sardines the manufacturer can squeeze into a tin, the greater his profit.

Whatever Next!

A prisoner in a German gaol literally chewed his way to freedom in 1907. The prisoner was Hans Schaarschmidt, who was serving a six-year sentence for robbery. The prison was a decaying fortress in Gera, whose windows were barred with pairs of crossed heavy wooden beams. Each day Schaarschmidt chewed away as much as his teeth could stand, then, to avoid suspicion, he filled in the holes in the beams with a rubbery paste made from the bread he was fed. After three months, Schaarschmidt was able to remove the bread putty and squeeze through to freedom.

An octopus has three hearts.

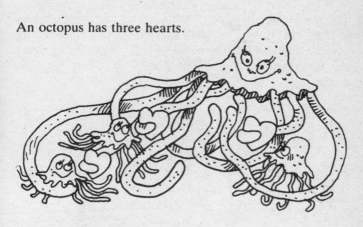

The Chinese language contains no "R" sounds; so the Chinese substitute the "L" sound for English words. On the other hand, the Japanese language has no "L" sound; they substitute an "R" sound. Thus in Chinese, "Fry" is pronounced "Fly"—and in Japanese, the word "Fly" is pronounced "Fry".

Man Talk

In 1982, intrepid-90 year-old Thompson Hora of Gosforth, Newcastle, made fifteen flights on a hang-glider.

Hang in there Grandpa

Lord Nelson, Britain's greatest admiral, suffered from acute sea-sickness throughout his life.

Anthony Ashill, a watch-repairer of Kidderminster in Worcestershire, ran an electric motor for over six months powered by a lemon.

Leonardo da Vinci could write with one hand while drawing with the other. You try.

When Charles, the Prince of Wales, wants to make a booking or travel incognito, to avoid fuss and an avalanche of publicity, he uses the pseudonym Mr Percy Perkins.

Ernest Digwood, of Leeds, Yorkshire, who died during the hot summer of 1976, left £26,000 to Jesus Christ, provided that He claims it before the year 2056.

Professor Rask, of Copenhagen University, could speak 235 languages fluently. He also compiled and published 28 different language dictionaries.

By the time his career in films had ended, crazy Keystone Cop Snub Pollard had been hit in the face with more than 20,000 custard pies.

How Weird!

Sultan Murad IV inherited 240 wives when he assumed the throne of Turkey in 1744. He decided to dispense with their services by the simple method of putting each wife in a sack and tossing them one by one into the Bosphorus.

Diovanni Rossi, an Italian miniature carver, once carved a collection of saints—in which 70 heads can be clearly seen—on a cherry stone.

Birmingham has 22 more miles of canal than Venice.

It's impossible to fold a piece of paper—no matter how big it is—more than seven times.

Kippers

Human beings are the only animals to sleep on their backs.

Like many Victorians, the novelist Charles Dickens ensured himself of a good night's sleep by keeping the head of his bed aligned precisely with the North Pole, so that the earth's magnetic force would pass longitudinally through his body. Using similar logic. Islamic worshippers point their beds towards Mecca.

Benjamin Disraeli was an insomniac and a believer in the occult.He was never able to fall asleep at night unless the four legs of his bed were planted in dishes filled with salt, to keep devilish spirits from attacking him.

Famous American soldier and president Dwight D. Eisenhower had ten pairs of pyjamas with the five stars of a general on them.

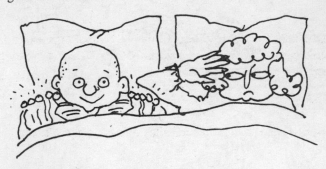

The average person changes position anywhere from 20 to 65 times in the course of a night's sleep.

Fire! Fire!

On a May morning in 1921, A. V. Bonham, of Haywards Heath, Sussex, saw smoke. He was startled to learn that it was his own house on fire. Apparently, Bonham's eleven year-old son had used paraffin to start a bonfire, and an explosion that followed had set the house aflame.

With the aid of neighbours, Bonham removed most of his household goods, but forgot about his loaded revolver which lay in a bureau drawer. As Bonham stood sadly watching the hungry flames, a shot rang out. At the same instant Bonham cried out, "I am shot!" and, clutching his chest, he staggered a few steps and then fell dead. The heat had exploded Bonham's own gun, and the bullet had found his heart.

Loopy Loos

In 1869, a patent was filed in London for a lavatory seat that had tiny rollers on the top to prevent anyone from standing on it.

On one of the Royal Family's trips to Canada, a ship's steward sold forty-four sheets of Royal Lavatory Paper to newspaper reporters for a dollar a sheet.

The 88-year-old public lavatory in Hayfield, Derbyshire, has now been turned into an ice-cream kiosk.

Potty Peers

William John Cavendish Bentinck Scott, the 5th Duke of Portland, who lived in the nineteenth century, must have been the shyest person who ever lived. For a short while he occupied his inherited seat in the House of Lords, but he soon found he was too timid to take part in the debates. So at twenty he retired to his estate and withdrew further and further into himself. The Duke eventually shut himself off in one corner of his home, Welbeck Abbey. He refused to receive visitors, and he wouldn't even see his own servants. All communications with him were passed through a message-box outside his door. Then the Duke had a tunnel dug from Welbeck Abbey to the town of Worksop, one and a half miles away. Later, he had additional tunnels dug to his greenhouse and other outbuildings, eliminating any encounters with anybody during short walks. He lived in this way for another fifty years, dying, a virtual recluse, at the age of seventy.

Viscount Castlereagh, one of the keenest intellects and greatest statesmen of the Napoleonic period, started acting rather strangely at the age of forty-seven, in 1815. One one occasion he knelt before King George IV and confessed to all manner of crimes, including treason, and the murder of Lord Palmerston—who was in the room at the time! He complained to the Speaker of the House of Commons that the House was empty when it was nearly full, and he would deny the existence of a piece of paper that he held in his hand. It seemed that years of hard work and worry had affected his brain. King George sent his own doctor to look after Castlereagh at his house in North Cray, Kent. His razors and guns were removed, but-nonetheless he committed suicide by cutting his throat with a pair of nail scissors in 1822.

Horse Sense

Early Victorian tram-hauling steam engines were disguised as horses, so as not to frighten the real horses in the streets.

Statues of famous people on horseback can tell you a lot about the rider. If the horse has all hooves on the ground, it means the rider died a natural death. If the horse has one foot in the air and three on the ground, the rider died of wounds. Two hooves in the air and two hooves on the ground means he was killed in action.

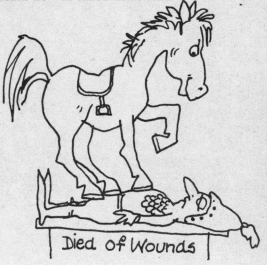

Died of Wounds

A racehorse can be a "one-year-old" just a few minutes after its birth. This is because it becomes one year old on January 1st following its birth—so if it's born just before midnight on December the 31st, if gains a whole year.

Nutty Numbers

170,141,183,460,469,229,731,687,303,715,884,105,727 is the largest number that cannot be divided by any other.

142857 is something of a mystic number. All the figures of the sum appear when multiplied as follows:

142857 × 2 = 285714
142857 × 3 = 428571
142857 × 4 = 571428
142857 × 5 = 714285
142857 × 6 = 857142

But thereafter, a completely different result appears:

142857 × 7 = 999999

I'm thoroughly mystified

The most persistent number, mathematically, is: 526,315,789,473,684,210. You may multiply this figure by any number you choose, but the original figures will always appear in the result.

The Indian ruler Khanjahan enjoyed handshaking with his subjects so much that when he died he left orders to be buried in a conical tomb—with his hand stuck out through the wall. Every visitor to the tomb shook hands with the corpse. Eventually, 35 years later, the hand withered away.

The famous spiritualist Amy Semple MacPherson was buried with a live telephone in her coffin.

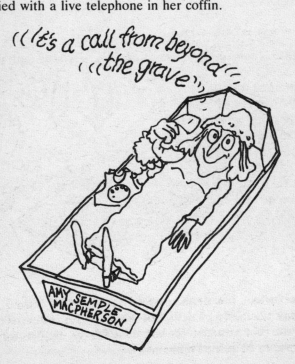

Margaret Thompson, a wealthy London socialite of the eighteenth century, had a passionate fondness for sneezing. When she died in 1776, her will directed that she should be buried in a coffin packed with snuff. She named the six most prodigious snuff-takers in London to be her pall-bearers, and they were instructed to wear snuff-coloured suits and beaver hats as they carried her remains to the cemetery. Six maidens preceded the cortege, inserting snuff into their own nostrils, distributing quantities of fine Scottish snuff to onlookers every twenty yards, and scattering snuff to the four winds like rose petals. The minister, for his services, and continued prayers, was bequeathed one pound of best snuff.

The famous Elizabethan poet Ben Jonson is buried in a sitting position in Poet's Corner at Westminster Abbey, for the plot provided for him wasn't large enough for the corpse to be placed horizontally.

Boy Wonders

Mozart wrote the music of "Twinkle, Twinkle Little Star" at the age of five.

John Trundley, known as the "Great Fat Lad of Peckham Rye", was born in 1899. At the age of eleven he weighed 178 kilograms (28 stone).

Thomas Young, the 18th century physician, mathematician and scientist, could speak twelve languages fluently at the age of eight.

Ten-year-old, Abdullah Lassar, the son of a rich Arabian oil magnate, received £575 pocket money a week.

Who'd Have Thought It?

A 55-year-old Polish man, Jan Dbworski, died in Stoke-on-Trent in 1966 from choking on a garlic clove he had left in his mouth overnight to ward off vampires.

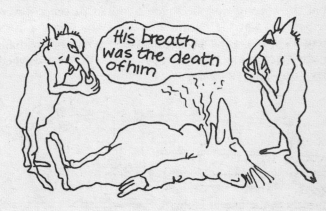

On the 24th August, 1918, in Hendon, near Sunderland, it rained eels for ten minutes. The fish covered about half an acre.

A Russian woman, Eva Vassilet, gave birth to 16 pairs of twins, 7 sets of triplets, and 4 sets of quads—a grand total of 69 children.

Denis Taverstock, of Lancashire, compiled a complete pack of playing cards by picking them up in the street. After collecting for 10 years, he was only 15 cards short. But it took him another 21 years finally to complete the pack in 1890.

What's Cooking?

A passenger train in Cordoba, Argentina, was derailed in 1971 when it struck and killed a cow that was lazing about on the track. Nobody was injured (apart from the cow), but the appetites of the seven hundred passengers were apparently whetted by the accident. While waiting for a repair crew to arrive and set the train on its way again, the passengers dug a barbecue pit, roasted the cow over a large fire, and devoured it with gusto.

The science of cooking a hamburger is now officially known as Hamburgerology.

Good Mourning

Black isn't the universal colour for mourning the dead. South Sea Islanders wear red; Ethiopians wear brown; Egyptians wear yellow; and the people of Turkey wear violet.

Wallpaper was first used as a decoration for Chinese tombs.

Some Tibetans have the custom of chopping up their dead relatives and feeding them to the birds.

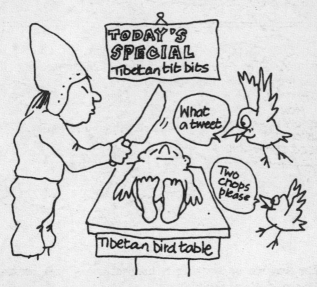

What's in a Name?

Among the curious names listed in the New York telephone directory are: Mona Lisa Gooseberry, Oscar Asparagus, Peculiar Smith, Sistine Madonna McClung, Virgin Mary Smith, and Lizzie Izabitchie.

The late Western Empress Dowager, of China, was named: Tzuh-hsi-tuan-yu-chuang-chen-shou-klung-chin-hsein-chung-hsi-huang-tai-hou.

Lady Macbeth had a son called Lulach the Fatuous.

The longest name yet given to a child was bestowed on the daughter of Arthur Pepper, a Liverpool laundryman, in 1924. The child's initials used up the whole alphabet, and her christening occupied half a day. They called her: Anna Bertha Cecelia Diana Emily Fanny Gertrude Hypatia Inez Jane Kate Louise Maud Nora Ophelia Prudence Quince Rebecca Sarah Teresa Ulysis Venus Winifred Xenephon Yetty Zeno Pepper. She was usually called Alpha Pepper for short.

The famous artist Picasso's full name was: Pablo Diego Jose Francisco de Paula Juan Nepomuceno Maria de los Remedios Cipriano de la Santissima Trinidad Ruiz Picasso.

The last name in the Chicago, USA, phone directory is Zeke Zzzyot.

Edible Entertainment

Those gimmick-crazy Japanese have invented an amazing kind of pop record. When you get bored with it, you can sprinkle it with milk and sugar and eat it. It's made of compressed rice.

Your morning newspaper is chock-full of cellulose, which is rich in carbohydrates. While carbohydrates in excess are not very good food value. Dr Steinkraus of the Swiss Agricultural Experimental Station in Geneva has pointed out that 450 kilograms of these carbohydrates, if fermented properly, can be turned into 5,000 kilograms of body-building protein. Properly processed newsprint, he says, will be of great value as the world's food supplies dwindle over the centuries. Though somehow it sounds a little unappetising to draw your chair up to the table, put on your napkin and tuck into a big bundle of last week's Daily Mirrors . . .

Regarding Reptiles

A snake at London Zoo was fitted with a glass eye.

Despite the expression "crocodile tears", crocodiles never cry or shed tears.

Snakes hear through their jaws.

The Mountain Devil, a lizard-like creature that lives in Australia, never drinks. It absorbs tiny drops of dew through its skin.

It is against the law to eat snakes on Sunday in Iraq.

My Word!

"Machoumaerobilengmonoolemongametsoarobilengmo-
noolemong" means "99" in the language of the Basuto
tribe of Africa.

An advertisement for cough syrup in a French newspaper
read:
"PARAMINOBENZOYLDIAETHYLAMI-
NOAETHANALOMPHYDROCHLORICUM ought to
be in everybody's medicine cabinet!"

Here is the world's longest swear word (you'll have to
work out the meaning for yourself)—it is, of course, in
German:
"Himmelherrgottkreuzmillionendonnerwetter!"

In Connecticut, U.S.A., there is Lake Chagoggagogg-manchuagogchaubunagungaamaug". In the Red Indian language this means: "You fish on your side; I fish on my side—nobody shall fish in the middle."

The longest-named railway station in the world is in North Wales. It is:
LLANFAIRPWLLGWYNGYLLGOGORYCHWYRN-DROBWLLLLANTYSILIOGOGOCH. (The station's nameplate, by the way, is 24 metres long.)

The longest word in the English language is not, as most people seem to think:
"ANTIDISESTABLISHMENTARIANISM"
This is just a junior at 28 letters long. The record is in fact a word that's 48 letters long, describing a lung disease, namely:
"PNEUMONOULTRAMISCROSCOPICICSILICO-VOLCANOCONIOSIS"

Greedy Guts

At the opening of the new city workhouse in Southampton in 1832, the lecture given to the assembled paupers was an hour and a half's talk on "Thrift".

The dinner given for the V.I.Ps attending the workhouse opening included the following: lobster, roast chicken, ham, veal patties, tongue, wine jellies, cherry tarts, savoy cakes, and eleven different kinds of wine.

For the inmates, however, the fare was a little more restricted: bread and lard, bread and margarine, unsweetened cocoa.

Lord Edward Russell gave a party in London in 1807 where 6,000 men got drunk. A large fountain was used as a punch bowl, into which 800 gallons of brandy were poured. Other ingredients included 70 gallons of rum, 20,000 lemons, 1,400 pounds of sugar, and 50 nutmegs.

20-year-old Sandy Allen, the world's tallest woman at 7 feet 5 inches (2.26m.) had her first date when a 7 foot 2 inch man drove all the way from Illinois to Indiana to take her out. For dinner, Sandy had ten shrimp cocktails, six large steaks, a triple banana split and eight double portions of ice-cream cake.

Batty Battles

A war fought between England and Zanzibar, which began on the 27th August 1896, lasted just 38 minutes.

During the Battle of Rancagua in October, 1814, the Chilean patriot Bernado O'Higgins commanded a badly outnumbered army. The revolutionaries were surrounded by Spanish troops and were running low on ammunition. O'Higgins himself was wounded. There seemed to be no hope of fighting their way out of a desperate situation.

Then O'Higgins ordered his men to gather up every animal in the village—dogs, horses, cows, sheep, even ducks and chickens. With their remaining ammunition, the troops scared the animals into a frantic stampede. Mooing, barking, braying, the motley menagerie charged towards the enemy lines, scattering the terrified Spaniards in all directions. O'Higgins and his men took advantage of the confusion to ride through the breach and escape to freedom.

Games for a Laugh

Here's an odd cricket statistic that's unlikely to be repeated: In the 1980 English tour of Australia, the English player Willey bowled to a player named Lillie, who was promptly caught by a player named Dilley.

In 1912, a woman golfer at Shawnee, Pennsylvania, misjudged her shot and sliced her ball into the Delaware River. Her husband rowed her after it while she took shot after shot, sending up great fountains of water, trying to reach it. Eventually, after struggling for an hour, she landed the ball one and a half miles away, and then had to play it all the way back to the green. Her total for this hole (the sixteenth) was a record-breaking hundred and fifty-six strokes. Shortly after this she gave up golf for horse riding.

Hot Dogs

At an open-air concert in Juarezeiro do Norte, Brazil, in the summer of 1973, a singer named Waldick Sorano was giving a performance of a humorous song called "I Am Not A Dog". Suddenly, halfway through the song, a dog trotted on stage, wearing a large sign that read "I Am Not Waldick Sorano". Infuriated by the practical joke, Sorano chased the dog offstage and started insulting the audience, who were in fits of laughter. The audience retaliated by slinging rotten peaches and tomatoes at him. A free-for-all fight ensued, and Sorano was forced offstage and chased all the way back to his hotel room.

Upon being crowned Queen of England, Victoria's very first royal proclamation was a command that all her dogs be given a hot bath. Queen Victoria owned up to eighty dogs at a time, and knew them all by name.

Family Affairs

Edwin Wakeman, of Manchester, committed suicide in 1927, leaving behind him the following note:

I married a widow with a grown daughter.

My father fell in love with my step-daughter and married her—thus becoming my son-in-law.

My step-daughter became my step-mother because she was my father's wife.

My wife gave birth to a son, who was, of course, my father's brother-in-law, and also my uncle, for he was the brother of my step-mother.

My father's wife became the mother of a son, who was, of course, my brother, and also my grandchild, for he was the son of my step-daughter.

Accordingly, my wife was my grandmother, because she was my step-mother's mother. I was my wife's husband and grandchild at the same time.

And, as the husband of a person's grandmother is his grandfather, I am my own grandfather!

Small wonder the confused Mr Wakeman did himself in.

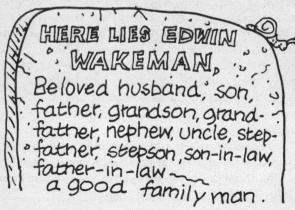

HERE LIES EDWIN WAKEMAN, Beloved husband, son, father, grandson, grandfather, nephew, uncle, step-father, stepson, son-in-law, father-in-law— a good family man.

Ah-Kwei, of Kansu, China, was a great-great-great-great-great-great-great-great-grandfather! He lived to see his descendants down to the tenth generation. He was presented to the son of the son of the son of the son of the son of the son of the son of the son of the son of *his* son! Ah-Kwei lived in the Golden Age of Happiness. And when the Emperor of China was searching for the happiest man in his empire, the Kansu patriach was brought before him.

In 1790, Ah-Kwei had a hundred and thirty-five living great-great-great-great-great-great-great-great grandchildren. One shudders at the thought of his Christmas present bill!

Moo!

The energy released by the heat of a cow's belches in just one day would be sufficient to generate central heating in an average-sized house for over a week.

Bulls are colour-blind.

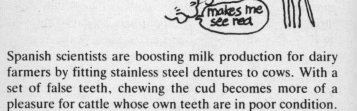

Spanish scientists are boosting milk production for dairy farmers by fitting stainless steel dentures to cows. With a set of false teeth, chewing the cud becomes more of a pleasure for cattle whose own teeth are in poor condition. The cows' milk yield has soared by up to 70 per cent.

Revving It Up

The people of the village of Holyrood Ampney, in Gloucestershire, petitioned the House of Commons in 1855 to have their vicar excommunicated. The parson in question had the somewhat ill-fitting name of Benedict Grace. For in their petition, the villagers alleged that the Rev. Grace was: "a most unholy type of man. He is much given to drunkenness, shouting, and chasing young girls about the parish. Furthermore, the parson is uncivil, ignorant, uncharitable, lewd, cruel, and uses filthy un-Christian language . . ." The petition was successful, for the Rev. Benedict Grace disappeared shortly afterwards.

Baptising an infant in 1971, the Rev Spinney, of Meltham, in the West Riding of Yorkshire, dipped his fingers into the holy water and scooped out six pork chops.

Fish and Ships

Five piranha fish could easily chew up a horse and its rider in 7 minutes, leaving behind just a skeleton horse with a skeleton rider.

S.S. *Cardiff*, a merchantman laden with a twin cargo of timber and tapioca powder, was about to dock at Cardiff in South Wales in October, 1974, when the timber caught fire. The crew confined the fire to one hold by wetting down the wood, but the fire brigade on shore drenched the ship with thousands of gallons of water. This seeped into the holds where the tapioca was stored, turning the powder into a watery gruel which was then cooked by the heat from the blazing timber. The ever-swelling ocean of syrupy tapioca pudding threatened to burst the ship's hull, and a fleet of lorries had to relieve the *Cardiff* of about seven million gallons of cooked tapioca.

When Sir Francis Drake's famous ship, the *Golden Hind*—in which he had sailed around the world—arrived back in London in 1580, the nation went wild. It was seriously suggested that the ship should be set on top of the spire of St Paul's Cathedral (estimates for the task came to £10,000). Another scheme was that the *Golden Hind* be moored on the lawns of Buckingham Palace, or even housed inside the palace itself. However, these plans came to nought. The *Golden Hind* was left moored in the Thames at Deptford in London. Within two years it had been pulled to pieces by souvenir-hunters, and not a single splinter of it was left.

The archer fish of India catches insects by squirting water at them from its mouth and drowning them. It has a range of about 5 feet.

Feline Facts

In 1980 a Siamese cat called Lucky arrived safely at Heathrow airport after hiding in the hold of a Boeing 747 plane. During the twenty days she'd been there, she'd travelled all around the world twice.

Edgar Allan Poe, the master horror writer, wrote all his stories with his black cat "Magic" sitting on his shoulder.

Cat gut has nothing to do with cats at all. It comes from sheep.

Napoleon, Emperor of France and would-be ruler of the world, was terrified of cats, and would not enter a room that had one in it.

Protected Species

America has some strange laws to protect its wildlife and its tamelife. For instance, it is illegal to "mistreat or otherwise hurt the feelings" of oysters in Baltimore, Maryland. And "fish-lassooing" is prohibited in Knoxville, Tennessee.

In Arizona, kicking a mule (however stubborn) is a punishable offence. So is "deliberately worrying or chasing" squirrels in Topeka, Kansas. And in California, you are breaking the law if you pluck the feathers from a live goose.

A vegetarian postscript: vegetables have feelings too, you know. Since 1972, the Society for the Prevention of Cruelty to Mushrooms of Michigan has zealously guarded the best interests of mushrooms. Anybody plucking and eating mushrooms is liable to a fine or a telling-off by the Society's three thousand members.

Our Whacky World

In Japan, Santa Claus isn't a jolly old man—she's a jolly old woman.

The "Kyaik-Hto-Yo" pagoda in Burma is built on a huge boulder which stands on the brink of a 2,000 foot chasm. The local natives believe the boulder is balanced on a single hair from the head of Buddha.

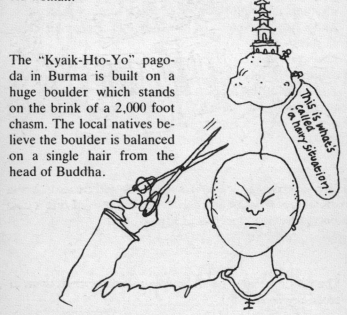

This is what's called a hairy situation!

Every summer evening on the German island of Sylt, the police go out on to the beaches and flatten children's sandcastles. No, they're not really spoilsports. The reason is that sand is very scarce there, and has to be imported, and sandcastles are easily washed away by the incoming tide.

A large road sign at the entrance to the town of Markle, Indiana, USA, states: Welcome To Markle, Home Of 902 Happy People And 4 Grouches.

When the city of St Pierre in Martinique was destroyed by an earthquake in 1908, only Augustia Ciparis, in jail for a minor offence, survived—out of a population of over 30,000 people.

Brazil used to print a bank note worth one cruzeiro. It was discontinued in 1960, when it was discovered that it cost one and a half cruzeiros to print.

The religion of the Todas people of India forbids them to cross any kind of bridge.

The Kirghiz tribe in Asia forbids a woman to utter her husband's name. The penalty for doing so is instant divorce.

Mr. Big

Honest Jack Fuller, a politician in the eighteenth century, was known by nearly everybody as The Hippopotamus, because of his vast size. Jack Fuller's appetite was prodigious; at a single sitting he could devour a whole hog's head, several pounds of beef, chicken, etc. and still have room for a whole five-pound chocolate pudding, a gallon of ale and a pint of claret. Fuller is buried in a fifteen-foot high pyramid in Brightling churchyard, Sussex—he is reputed to be at rest inside it sitting at a table with a bottle of claret before him and an eleven-course meal.